Drawing Dogs and Puppies

Drawing Dogs and Puppies

by Paul Frame

A HOW-TO-DRAW BOOK
FRANKLIN WATTS
NEW YORK | LONDON | 1978

Library of Congress Cataloging in Publication Data

Frame, Paul, 1913-
   Drawing dogs and puppies.

   (A How-to-draw book)
   SUMMARY: A step-by-step guide to drawing dogs
and puppies including a list of basic materials and
warm-up exercises to improve drawing technique.
   1. Dogs in art — Juvenile literature. 2. Drawing —
Technique — Juvenile literature. [1. Drawing —
Technique] I. Title.
NC780.F68   743'.69'74442   78-5289
ISBN 0-531-01452-5

Contents

to everyone who loves to draw —
it's the most fun you can have alone

Drawing
Dogs and
Puppies

Introduction

Almost anyone who really *wants* to learn to draw
can do so. And you learn to draw by drawing.
A few very talented ones will learn to do it beauti-
fully. Most of the rest of us will succeed to the
degree of our desire and concentration.

Compare your work with that of more ac-
complished artists for one reason only. To learn.
If their work seems much better than yours,
remember this: they have probably been drawing
for some part of every day for years before
you started. Don't be discouraged.

Not *everyone* on a soccer team is a star.
Not all tennis players are as good as Chris Evert.
If we accept that and go on to play as well as
effort and practice will allow, most of us will
get great satisfaction from this effort.

Most success, no matter the degree, is a
combination of two ingredients. Complete concentration on the task and a very strong desire
to improve your skill. No one, no matter how
talented, ever improved without *constant* practice.

Enough preaching. If you really want to learn
to draw, you can. Follow the suggested exercises
in this book and in a few weeks you will improve
your ability noticeably. The *more* you understand
something, the better you are able to overcome
any difficulties you have with it. This applies not
only to dogs, which are the subject of this book,
but to almost everything else you wish to draw.

Chapter 1
Getting Started

Your first step is to collect the tools and other materials you'll need. The following will serve you well to begin with. As you improve and increase your confidence, you will probably discover and begin to use a wider range of tools and materials. That's as it should be. But to begin with, follow these suggestions.

BASIC MATERIALS

1. *Drawing board.* Any rigid and smooth surface about 14 inches to 18 inches (35.6 to 46 cm) wide and 20 inches to 24 inches (51 to 61 cm) long will do. You can use a piece of ¼-inch (.6 cm) plywood, or glue together with Elmer's glue several pieces of thick industrial cardboard or three pieces of corrugated board. Be careful to alternate the ribbing.

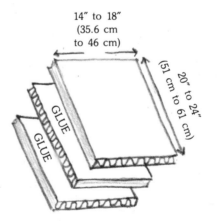

14″ to 18″
(35.6 cm to 46 cm)

20″ to 24″
(51 cm to 61 cm)

GLUE

GLUE

2. *Paper.* For practice sessions use large brown paper bags. Slit these down one side and at the bottom to get the largest surface, and if wrinkled, dampen slightly, then iron with a steam iron. Another source is the weekly laundry wrapping paper. If there isn't much from either of these sources in your house, perhaps the people next door or a local store will give you old wrappings.

If you feel rich, you can get 19-by-24-inch (48-by-61-cm) newsprint pads at your local artists' materials shop. But because you will use so much paper during these sessions, I advise using recycled sources and both sides of each piece.

When you are ready for more finished drawings, use any one of a number of drawing pads that can be bought at your local art supply, variety, or stationery store.

As you experiment with tools and materials, you will probably find the ones that feel right to you. It is always a good idea for any artist to try new tools and materials. Just be sure you become comfortable with your basic equipment first.

3. _Tools._ Start with **pencils**, preferably fairly soft leads — HB or 2B. If the weather is damp, your paper will be too. If so, you'll find 4B and 6B will feel better. Always keep a small pocket pencil-sharpener at hand.

If you prefer not to be sharpening your pencil constantly, perhaps an inexpensive automatic pencil will be the answer. Get the one that uses the so-called long lead. It comes in various grades up to 4B.

If the idea of a pencil that doesn't need to be sharpened appeals to you, there are also **lead holders** you can buy at any art supply store and any grade lead you can think of from 8H (very hard) to 6B (very soft).

press down to adjust or change lead

With these you'll want to keep a **sandpaper block** handy for making very sharp points. You can make your own block, using strips of 1-by-4-inch (2.5-by-10-cm) 00 fine sandpaper stapled to a piece of heavy cardboard. The sandpaper can be bought at the hardware store.

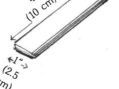

4" (10 cm)

1" (2.5 cm)

A **clip** is useful to hold the pad or loose paper to your drawing board. Clips can usually be had from your local stationery store.

Erasers are a must. It's better to have two kinds. The kneaded eraser is particularly useful for working in a very small area because it can be squeezed into any shape you need. It is also very good for making a line lighter in tone. Simply press on, then lift; don't rub the eraser on the area you want lighter. The eraser removes some of the surface lead. A plastic eraser is very good when you are working on large areas and when you want to remove all of the lead impressions, not just some of the tone.

Fixative will keep your drawings from smudging. Spray the ones you wish to save with Blair or Winsor and Newton workable fixative.

Tracing paper is a valuable tool. It comes in pads and will be needed for practice as explained in chapter 3.

4. Last but not least, get in the habit of carrying a **sketchbook** — one small enough to carry in your pocket. Make quick studies wherever and whenever you can, no matter how brief. This is excellent practice and you will find your sketchbooks will become as valuable to you as research notes are to an author.

REFERENCE FILE

There is something else you should begin immediately — a reference file of photographs and reproductions of fine artists' drawings of all the subjects that interest you. Artists often refer to this as a scrap file. Newspapers and magazines are very good sources for this kind of material. Go through and clip all the magazines that come into your home. If you'd like a wider selection, buttonhole all your friends and ask them to let you have all their family's old magazines. Then, to help finance your hobby, when you're finished clipping sell the old magazines to your local wastepaper dealer.

Keep your material in separate folders according to subject matter. Use this material when you cannot find a model, or when you want to study an action pose for a prolonged period.

Below is an example of a suggested breakdown. If you are interested in building a more extensive file, covering a wider range of subjects, write to me in care of the publisher. Enclose a self-addressed, stamped envelope and I will forward an outline for setting up a reference file.

Dogs: Active
Breed: German Shepherd (Alsatian)

Dogs: Passive
Breed: Poodle

ch with what

't worry that
e you express
at it even if
't be able to

es you, not
you are feeling
e at a time.

ser during
sessions are
some of each
. At the end of
a day, spread
re doing.

Chapter 2
Exercises

Each time you sit down to draw, it would be wise to have a warm-up period. These warm-up periods will be useful for the same reasons such activity is useful to musicians or athletes. They get your mind really concentrating on your subject, and this of course makes your hand and your mind begin to act together.

The length of these sessions can vary according to your own schedule. Try two ten-minute sessions — the first session for contour drawing, the second ten minutes for gesture drawing. Use a 2B pencil or lead.

Contour drawing. Use the paper bags or newsprint pad for this. Pick a simple familiar subject near at hand — your radio, a telephone, a bottle, or a piece of fruit, something that isn't too complex. Concentrate on the main elements only.

Sit fairly close to your subject. Now focus your eyes on some starting point along the contour (outline) of the subject. Placing your pencil on the

paper, imagine your pencil point is a[c]
ing and tracing the outline.

Now begin to move your eyes v[e]
along the outline, looking only at the
at your paper. This will not be easy
You'll be strongly tempted to look at
to check what your pencil is doing.

Be strong, resist, don't look. As
literally inches along the contour, mo
cil at the same slow pace, always try
the edge.

Remember, *don't* lift the pencil o
paper until you have finished the con
are contouring a subject that has are
contour and you wish to do them, lift
place it in the proper starting point
and start again.

the model looks like, or even so m
it is — but with what it is *doing*.

If you draw a dog running, dor
its head is not right. Just make sur
the motion, so that when you look
you don't know it's a dog, you wor
miss the forward rush of motion.

If you draw a person
leaning over, concen-
trate on showing the
curve of the head,
the extended hand.
Here again you don't
lift your pencil off the
surface. Let it move freely
around the paper. Don't be
concerned about detail.
Doing the opposite of
contour drawing, you
don't try to follow
the edges. Here you're
reporting the *feeling* the subject giv
its precise form. In gesture drawing
the whole thing at once, not a piec

Important point. Do not use an era
either one of these sessions. These
strictly training time. Save and date
type of drawing for future reference
two weeks of, say, twenty minutes
them out by date and see how you

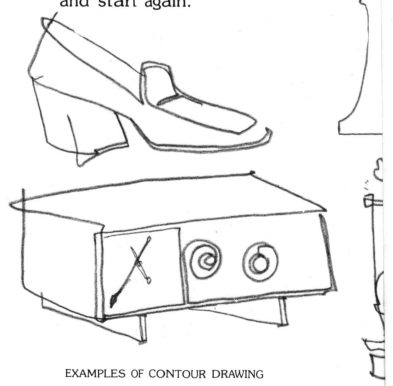

EXAMPLES OF CONTOUR DRAWING

(18)

Chapter 3
Understanding Proportions

Let's assume you now feel ready to start sketching dogs.

Use a simple block-construction method, shown on page 24, at this stage. The more complex method requires knowledge of both bone and muscle structure, which is something you may want to study later.

The skeletons below will give you some understanding of the dog. It is also very interesting to compare the structure of a dog to that of a human.

One key point to note is that a dog walks on its toes.

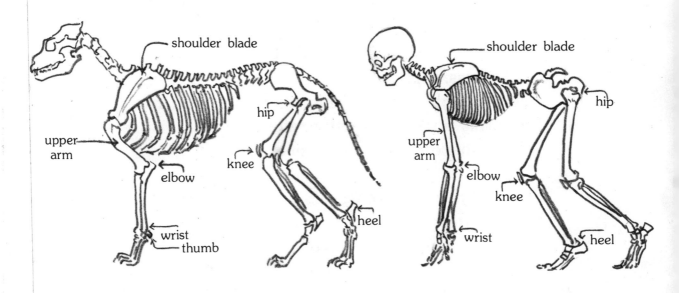

DOG **HUMAN**

These next few pages deal with the basic parts of the dog. They point out certain shapes that are characteristic of dogs — of all animals actually.

Below are illustrated the basic parts of an animal. Four legs, the trunk (or torso), and the neck and head.

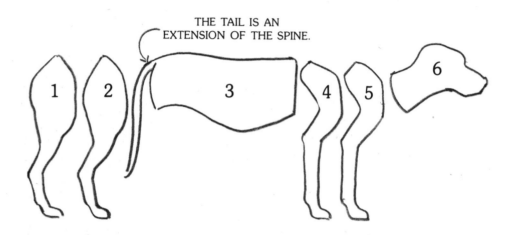

THE TAIL IS AN EXTENSION OF THE SPINE.

Proportions will vary slightly, sizes will vary considerably with the different breeds, and most certainly in the case of puppies. However the *basic* shape remains the same.

To help you further understand a dog's anatomy, the following general rules of proportion should keep you from going too far off course.

The trunk of most breeds measures the same from chest to rump as the front leg from footpad to top of the shoulder.

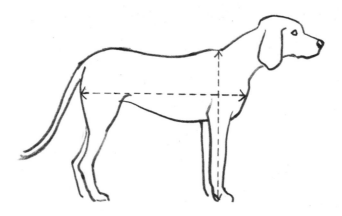

The most notable exceptions are those breeds with elongated trunks — the basset and the dachshund. Their trunks tend to run twice as long as the foreleg from pad to top of shoulder.

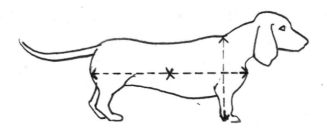

There are proportions governing the head as well. But remember, these are not hard and fast rules or mathematically exact. They are only guides.

In profile, from the tip of the muzzle to the eyes is almost half the length of the head. From stop (eye area) to occiput (back of head) is about a nose longer.

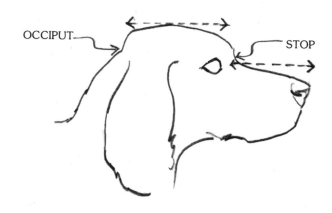

The space between the eyes is about double the width of the nose.

These guidelines are helpful, but don't become dependent on measurements. Study your reference photos, note the placement of each feature and its relationship to the others.

Now that you are armed with some basic information, start sketching using the simple blocking-in method.

You should really try drawing the whole dog first. However, since almost every beginner wants to do the head first, it will be explained first.

Four important points to remember are:

1. Pick a sharp-focus, profile photo of a dog, if possible short-haired. Long-haired dogs are more difficult for the beginner.

2. Sketch only the simplest forms first. *Do not* try to shade in these first sessions.

3. Check with the photo constantly to see if you are getting the proper relationship between parts of the head — eye to ear, and so on.

4. *Do not* think in terms of outline. You are *not* drawing an outline. You are enclosing a form. Always think of the other side even if you can't see it.

As mentioned earlier, save one or two of your sketches from each session. Date them, and in a month review them. You will learn much from this practice.

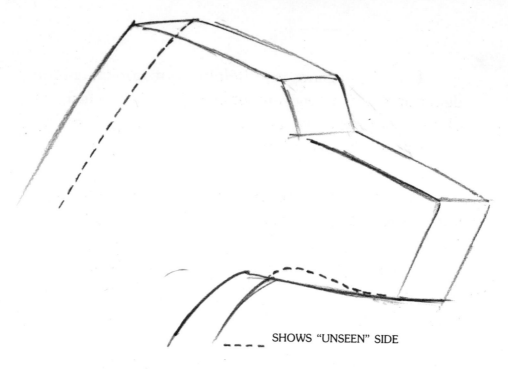

- - - - SHOWS "UNSEEN" SIDE

The sketch above is not a true profile. It is a shallow three-quarter view to show the concept of "seeing through." The sketch below looks down on the head. After you've sketched the above simple blocking-in several times, try the one below. If you can find a photo with this point of view, use that as a model.

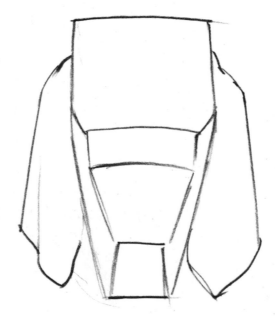

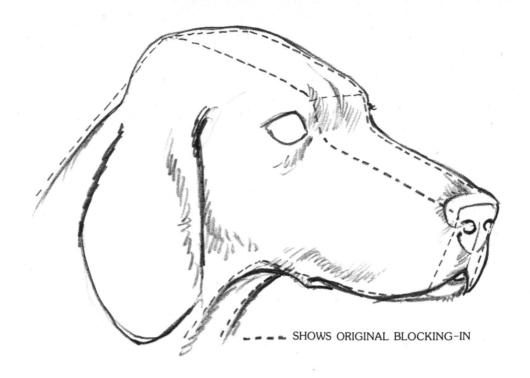

- - - - - SHOWS ORIGINAL BLOCKING-IN

Get out your tracing pad and use a piece of tracing paper to overlay *your* blocked-in sketch. Then, using it as a guide, make some of the refinements suggested on this page. If the refining doesn't go well, don't erase a lot. Start a new sketch.

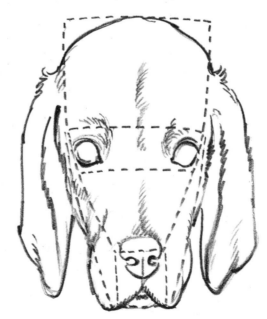

The next four
pages will show
eight different
heads. Each is in
the first two, sim-
plest stages of
development. Use
these as a guide
when sketching.

The ear placement
is very important.
While the ear is
always in the
same spot in the
skull, the differen-
ces in the shape
of the ear flap
can fool you.
Always make
careful note of
the relation-
ship between
the eye and
the ear.

After this sketch
the dotted line
indicating the first
stage will no
longer be shown.
Using a tracing
pad makes it
unnecessary.

The actual ear
opening in the
skull is here
beneath the skin.

The eye seems to change shape as the head moves.

FRONT VIEW
3/4 VIEW
PROFILE

This is best under-stood by using an egg. Draw a front view of an eye on the blunt end. Now turn the egg slowly and note the changes in the *appearance* of the shape.

Because of the different type of ear flap note the change in appearance of the ear.

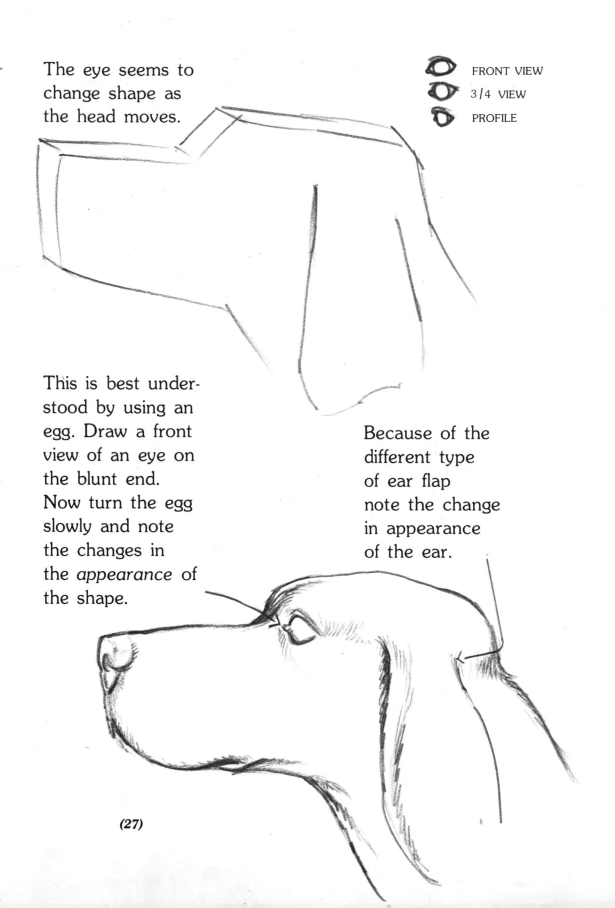

(27)

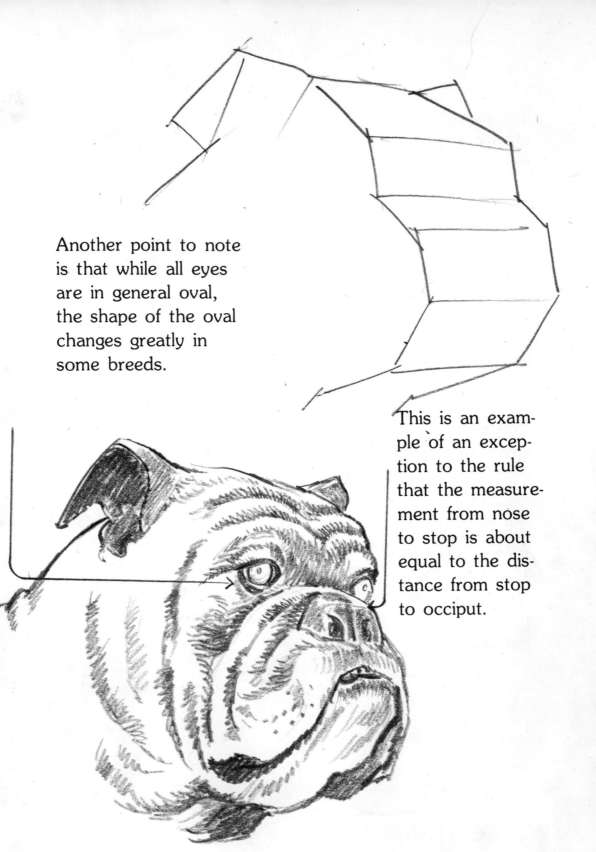

Another point to note
is that while all eyes
are in general oval,
the shape of the oval
changes greatly in
some breeds.

This is an exam-
ple of an excep-
tion to the rule
that the measure-
ment from nose
to stop is about
equal to the dis-
tance from stop
to occiput.

Note that the hair is longer at the back of the shepherd's neck and under its jaw. This tends to hide the true structure. You must observe even more carefully to understand the forms.

The heads on this and the next three pages are much more frontal. This will test your newfound awareness of dog anatomy and be more of a challenge for you.

These next four heads will also be a bit more finished. Try your hand at adding a few *simple* areas of shading.

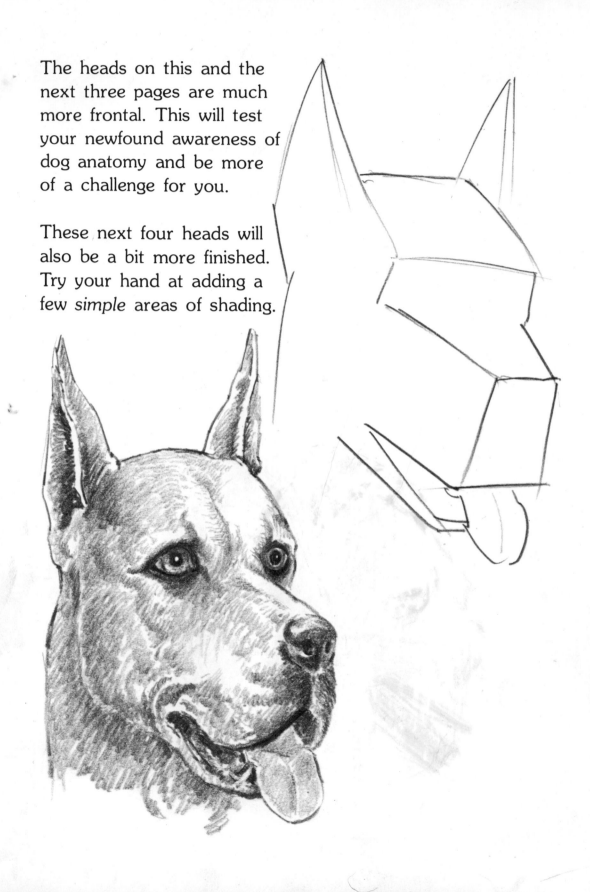

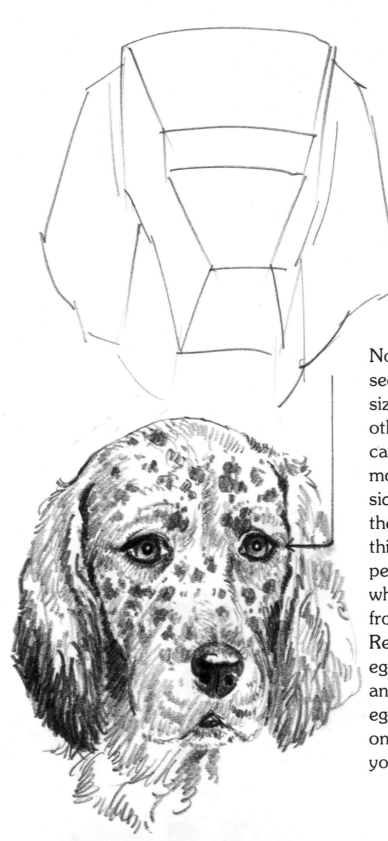

Note that this eye seems a different size from the other. This is because you see more of the left side of the head, therefore less of this eye. This happens to all forms when *not* seen from full front. Remember the egg? Go back and study the egg experiment on page 27 if you are unsure.

Foreshortening is the procedure used to make one part of an object appear to be nearer to you than another. Here on a flat surface you must make the nose and muzzle appear to be in front of the eyes and forehead. This effect and an understanding of how to achieve it must start at this first stage.

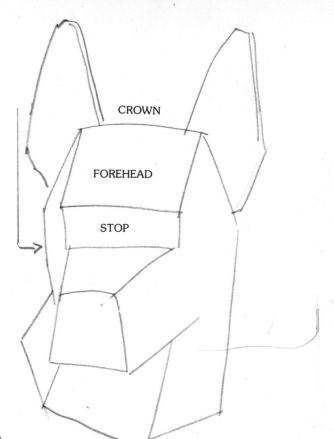

CROWN

FOREHEAD

STOP

Even in this more finished sketch, the darker nose and muzzle, and general indication of hair growth make the foreshortening only slightly more clear. So your basic blocking in is almost the most important part of your drawing. A house isn't much good if its foundation is badly built.

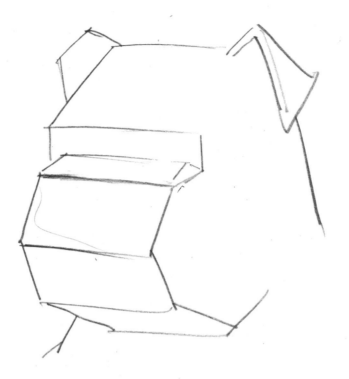

Here the foreshorten-
ing is not as difficult
to deal with. The trick
is to make the folds of
skin look like thick
folds of skin, not
just so many dark
and fuzzy lines. Be
sure to take a very
careful look at the
direction and intensity of
the lines indicating the hair.

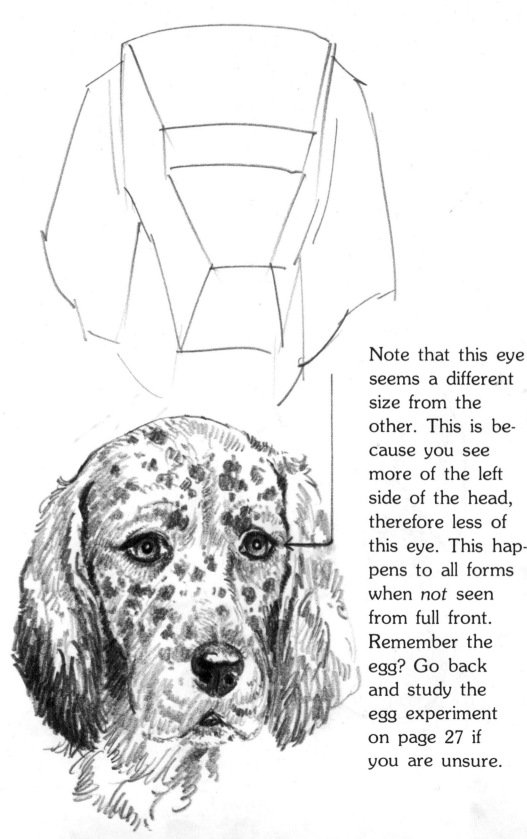

Note that this *eye* seems a different size from the other. This is because you see more of the left side of the head, therefore less of this eye. This happens to all forms when *not* seen from full front. Remember the egg? Go back and study the egg experiment on page 27 if you are unsure.

Foreshortening is the procedure used to make one part of an object appear to be nearer to you than another. Here on a flat surface you must make the nose and muzzle appear to be in front of the eyes and forehead. This effect and an understanding of how to achieve it must start at this first stage.

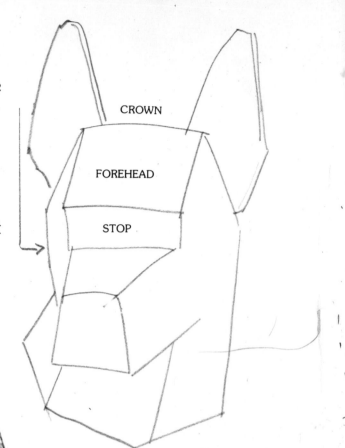

CROWN

FOREHEAD

STOP

Even in this more finished sketch, the darker nose and muzzle, and general indication of hair growth make the foreshortening only slightly more clear. So your basic blocking in is almost the most important part of your drawing. A house isn't much good if its foundation is badly built.

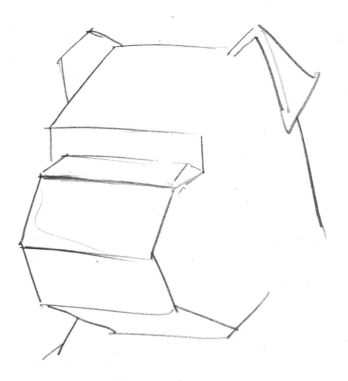

Here the foreshorten-
ing is not as difficult
to deal with. The trick
is to make the folds of
skin look like thick
folds of skin, not
just so many dark
and fuzzy lines. Be
sure to take a very
careful look at the
direction and intensity of
the lines indicating the hair.

Chapter 4
Sketching the Whole Dog —
Still and in Motion

This chapter deals with the dog as a whole.
You'll learn to block in the dog lying down,
sitting, and standing, in profile and three-quarter
views.

As with the head, it is all important to think
of the dog as a rounded form, *not* an outline.

Basically all forms are cylinders, made up of
curves, not straight lines. You've been using
straight lines to do your blocking in. They are the
easiest to use when you are trying to understand
how rounded forms are constructed.

If you have been working on the problems in
chapter 3, you should be able to go right into
using curved lines in your basic blocking in.

In these sketches you see a dog from several
points of view. This will open your eyes to how
the appearance of a form changes dramatically as
you move from one point of view to another.
Notice how foreshortened the whole body is. This
view may be difficult for you to draw until you
feel very sure of your understanding of anatomy.

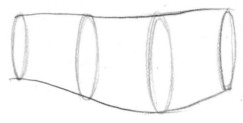

Until you are automatically thinking in terms of whole forms, continue your sketches as you see them here—as a sort of "see-through" drawing. Soon it will become second nature to you. Everything you see will have form and substance. Then you can leave out the "see-through" indications.

Remember the trunk of an animal is suspended between the four legs. It doesn't sit on top.

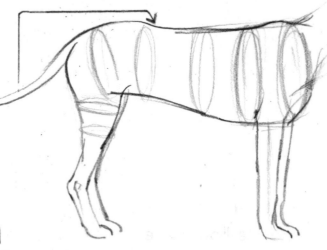

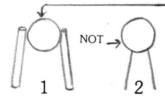

NOT →

1   2

Think of the trunk as shown in figure 1, never as in figure 2. Now fit the oval head on the neck cylinder, then both to the body cylinder. Eureka! The whole dog.

The big drawing
problems here are
the radical change
in the appearance
of the hindquarters
and the moderate
foreshortening of
the trunk and head.

You must realize
that this form is
in front of this.
Also note how these
same forms in the
shaded area look
very different. In
working on this view, you
must call on all your new
awareness of foreshortening
and careful observation.

Again note the
difference in the
same two forms
from another
point of view.

(37)

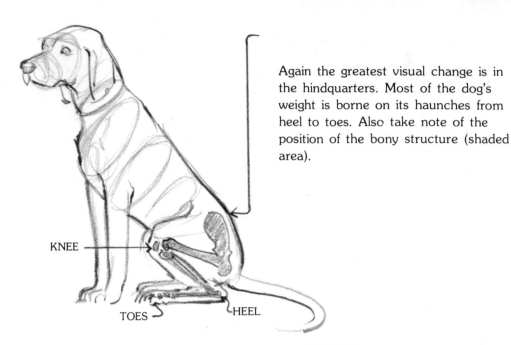

Again the greatest visual change is in the hindquarters. Most of the dog's weight is borne on its haunches from heel to toes. Also take note of the position of the bony structure (shaded area).

KNEE

TOES HEEL

The most important point to observe and place properly is the line of the spinal column (dotted line). It establishes the whole attitude of the dog. While all segments of an animal are important, the spinal column is one of the most important. You will see how true this is when you start drawing dogs in motion.

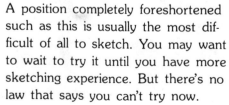

A position completely foreshortened such as this is usually the most difficult of all to sketch. You may want to wait to try it until you have more sketching experience. But there's no law that says you can't try now.

Using these three poses as an exercise demonstrates a point that must never be overlooked. With the slightest movement or change in point of view, all forms change dramatically.

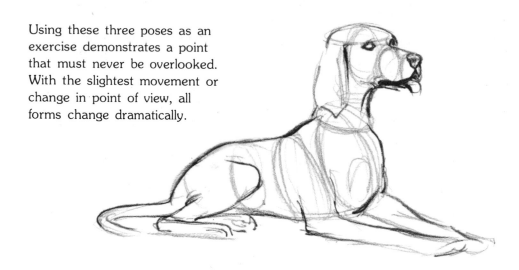

In these sketches the hindquarters change greatly even though the dog is using them in almost the same way in all three positions. Work with tracing paper over your blocking sketches until you feel you understand the basic form. Then sketch without tracing paper.

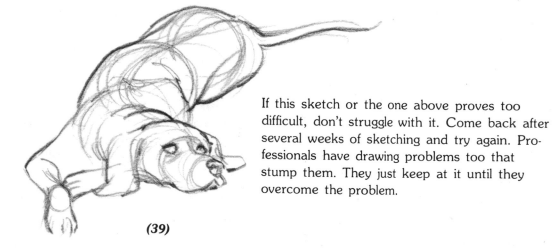

If this sketch or the one above proves too difficult, don't struggle with it. Come back after several weeks of sketching and try again. Professionals have drawing problems too that stump them. They just keep at it until they overcome the problem.

(39)

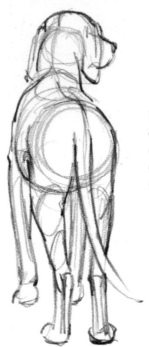

Using these three poses as an exercise emphasizes the point made on the preceding page. A slight movement by the dog or change in your point of view changes the form considerably.

In all three sketches a marked change takes place even though the basic pose changes very little. Use your tracing paper over your blocking in, refining each sketch as best you can.

If you find these sketches too difficult, don't worry. Try again after several weeks of practice. If they still are too difficult, keep working on them from time to time until you master the problem.

These are three different stages in a dog's walking gait. It is *not* an entire stride or walking sequence. However, it will give you an idea of some of the leg positions and the dog's general appearance.

In drawing a walking dog, having three paws on the ground at the same time looks most convincing. It's a moment when the dog seems well planted yet moving.

However, there is a moment in the walking sequence when just two legs are on the ground. At this time the weight is evenly distributed between the diagonal legs—those shaded and marked 1 and 2.

Here are three phases of a dog at the trot. In the trot each pair of diagonal legs (shaded and numbered) are lifted alternately.

Notice that even in the action of the walk and trot, the head does not change its position. This is true of the spine as well, so the sense of action must be conveyed by the legs.

This is the moment when all four feet are off the ground. It happens twice during each full stride. Use all of the action sketches as a guide in making your own action studies. It would be a good idea to substitute other kinds of dogs.

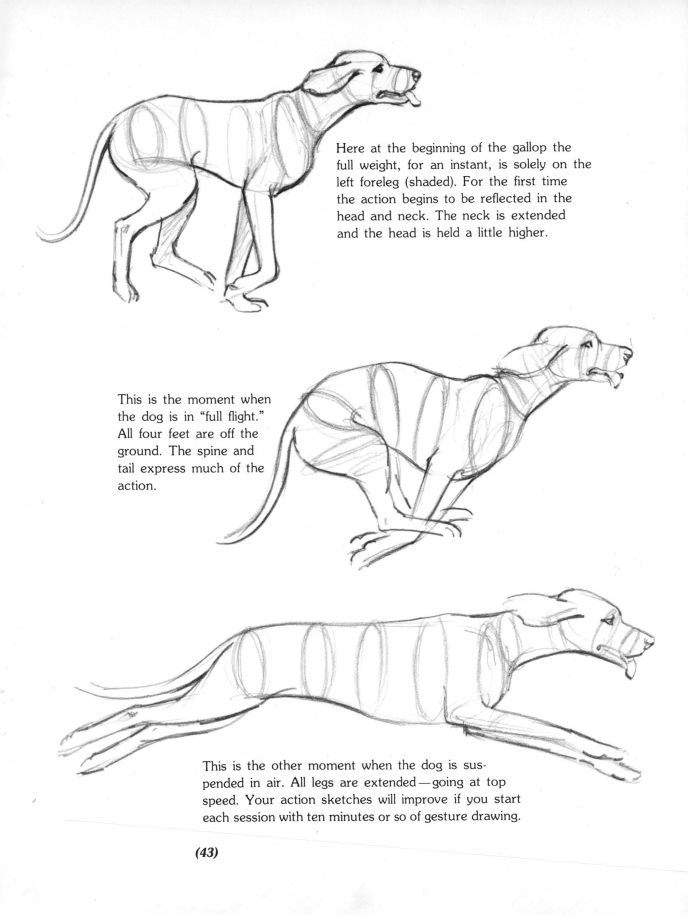

Here at the beginning of the gallop the full weight, for an instant, is solely on the left foreleg (shaded). For the first time the action begins to be reflected in the head and neck. The neck is extended and the head is held a little higher.

This is the moment when the dog is in "full flight." All four feet are off the ground. The spine and tail express much of the action.

This is the other moment when the dog is suspended in air. All legs are extended—going at top speed. Your action sketches will improve if you start each session with ten minutes or so of gesture drawing.

In summing up these past ten pages, there are four areas to be particularly aware of.

1. The line of the spine or backbone: If you can capture the true line of the action of the spine, your sketch will convey much of the basic feeling of the action.

2. The stretch and/or the arch of the neck: If this element is accurately observed and drawn — even a passive position — it will add greatly to the feeling of a sketch.

3. The legs: Always be careful to make them look as though they are bearing weight, stretching, or caught in motion.

4. The ears: The position of a dog's ears will indicate if the animal is alert or passive, angry or pleased. The ears frequently set the mood of a sketch.

Chapter 5
Light and Shade

In time you will want to start making more finished drawings. This will require shading. For shading you will need a working knowledge of light and shade.

To add this dimension to your sketches, read and work through this chapter carefully.

For the time being, you need only to consider two types of light:

Full light, which occurs wherever the form is fully exposed to the light source.

Shadow area, where the form or forms are to some degree removed from a direct light source.

In both figures A and B, full light hits side 1. In figure A, side 2 is partially removed from the light source. Side 3 in both A and B is almost totally removed from the light source. Therefore it is darkest of all.

In figure B, the difference is that the form is round, so the shading is more gradual. Figure B illustrates the sort of light problem you are most likely to have in working on your sketches. There will be very few hard edges.

LIGHT SOURCE

This head is oversimplified to make your first attempts a bit easier to understand.

Areas numbered 1 are receiving the most direct light, so they will be the lightest areas.

Everywhere the number 2 appears, the form is receiving partial light so those areas are darker in tone than areas marked 1.

The areas marked 3 get even less light, so they are a bit darker than areas marked 2.

The nose (partially because of its naturally darker tone), particularly the inside of the nostril and the inside of the upper lip, is your darkest tone.

Full understanding of light and shade requires much time and study. However, using the simple formula above will take care of your needs until you progress beyond what this book has to teach.

(46)

Hair patterns are a most important consideration when making more finished sketches of dogs.

The direction of hair growth combined with the tone and muscle beneath the hair make the basic forms. These in turn are emphasized by light and shade.

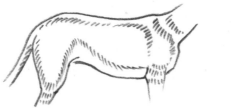

Figure A exposes muscle structure of part of the hindquarters. Figure B shows what it might look like when the same area is covered by skin and hair. The shadows are darkened to emphasize the point.

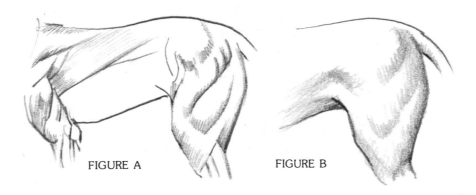

FIGURE A   FIGURE B

Understanding hair patterns and their variations, particularly in long-haired breeds, requires a lot of careful observation from life.

The sketch below further illustrates what takes place when light, shade, and hair patterns are combined in a sketch. The Afghan was chosen because in one head you have long and short hair.

Shade your sketch as shown. Use pencil strokes that follow the direction of the hair growth.

If you wish to darken an area, go over it again, pressing harder with a softer pencil. This has been done here particularly in the areas of the eye, the nose, and under the lower jaw.

From this page to page 54 there are three types of dog heads for you to use as a guide to sketching.

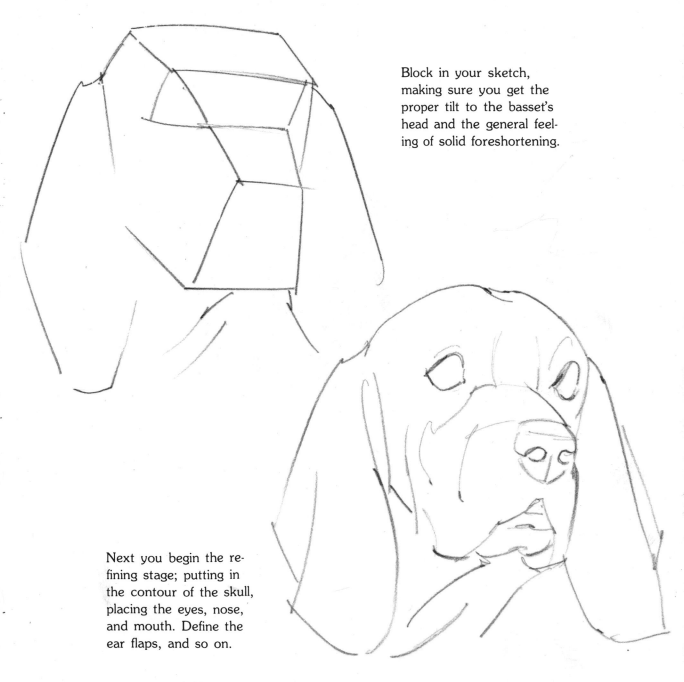

Block in your sketch, making sure you get the proper tilt to the basset's head and the general feeling of solid foreshortening.

Next you begin the refining stage; putting in the contour of the skull, placing the eyes, nose, and mouth. Define the ear flaps, and so on.

Next, lightly indicate the necessary details—the placement of tonal areas such as the dark eye patches, the ears, and lips. Then indicate where you want highlights, such as in the eyes, nose, and lips.

In finishing your sketch, it's better to establish your darkest tones first, then the next darkest areas. Doing it this way means you must plan ahead, and helps you keep better control of the shading. When doing large areas of tone such as the ears and eye patches, apply an all-over, even tone first. Then work in a select few details in a slightly darker tone to give added form.

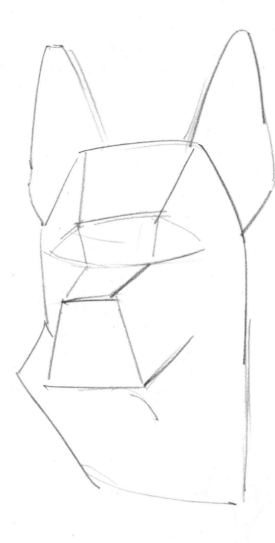

When blocking in the dog's head, the angle is again the most important thing to establish correctly. That and the ears give the look of alertness which is the key to the feeling of this head.

In refining, try not to lose any of the foreshortening in the muzzle. That is what conveys much of the character of the shepherd or Alsatian.

There are more areas of tone in this head than in the basset's so be careful to plan well. Don't get too complicated and become lost in a sea of lines and then wonder what they mean.

In this final stage the more complicated tonal problem can continue to cause you trouble. Try not to just copy this head. Study it carefully to understand what each tonal value does.

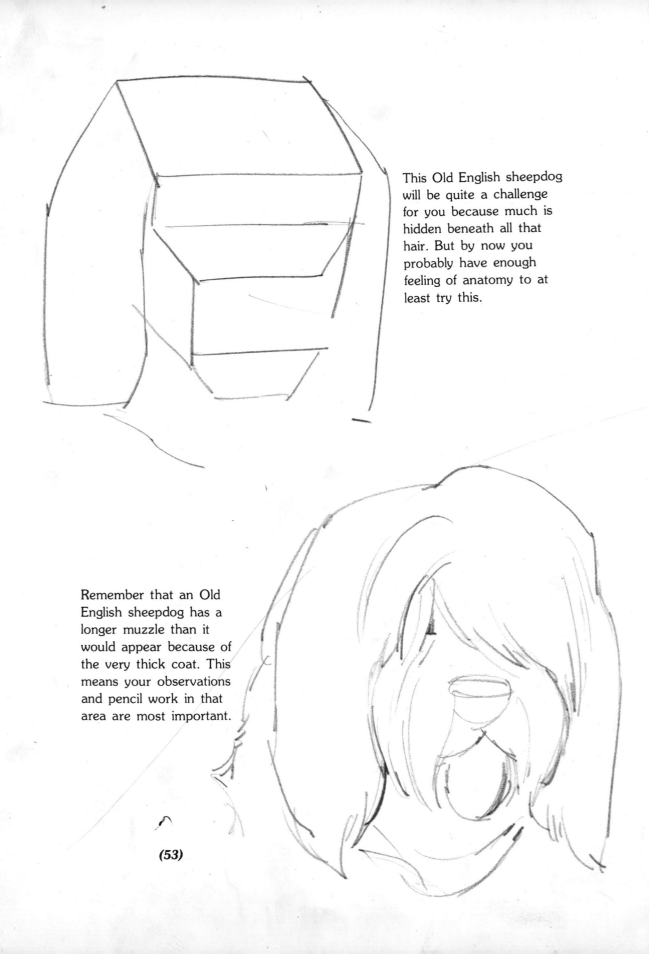

This Old English sheepdog will be quite a challenge for you because much is hidden beneath all that hair. But by now you probably have enough feeling of anatomy to at least try this.

Remember that an Old English sheepdog has a longer muzzle than it would appear because of the very thick coat. This means your observations and pencil work in that area are most important.

(53)

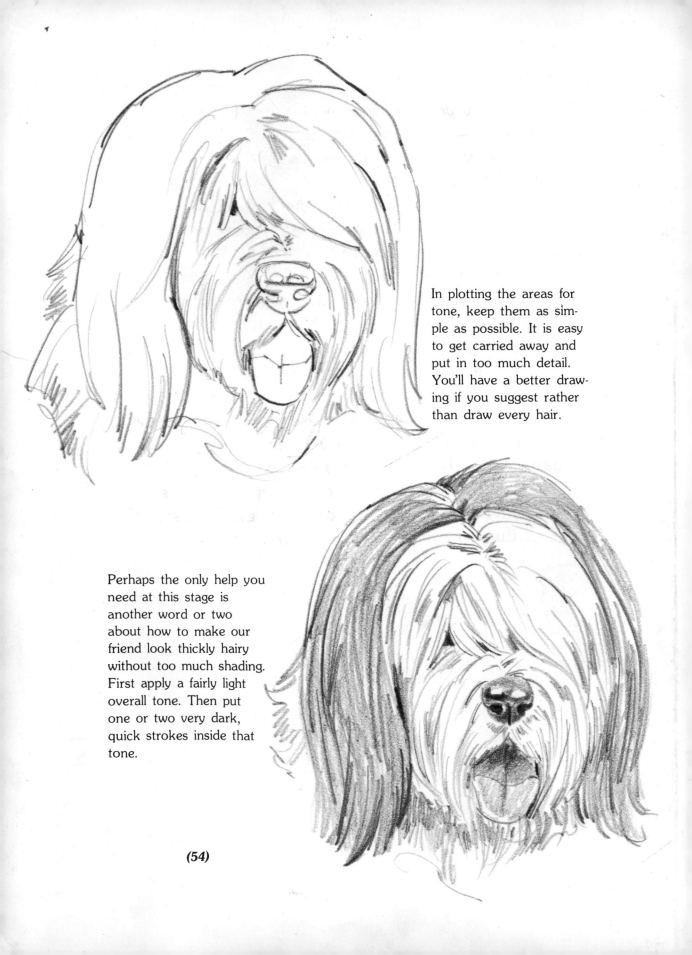

In plotting the areas for tone, keep them as simple as possible. It is easy to get carried away and put in too much detail. You'll have a better drawing if you suggest rather than draw every hair.

Perhaps the only help you need at this stage is another word or two about how to make our friend look thickly hairy without too much shading. First apply a fairly light overall tone. Then put one or two very dark, quick strokes inside that tone.

(54)

Chapter 2
Exercises

Each time you sit down to draw, it would be wise to have a warm-up period. These warm-up periods will be useful for the same reasons such activity is useful to musicians or athletes. They get your mind really concentrating on your subject, and this of course makes your hand and your mind begin to act together.

The length of these sessions can vary according to your own schedule. Try two ten-minute sessions — the first session for contour drawing, the second ten minutes for gesture drawing. Use a 2B pencil or lead.

Contour drawing. Use the paper bags or newsprint pad for this. Pick a simple familiar subject near at hand — your radio, a telephone, a bottle, or a piece of fruit, something that isn't too complex. Concentrate on the main elements only.

Sit fairly close to your subject. Now focus your eyes on some starting point along the contour (outline) of the subject. Placing your pencil on the

paper, imagine your pencil point is actually touching and tracing the outline.

Now begin to move your eyes very slowly along the outline, looking only at the subject not at your paper. This will not be easy to do at first. You'll be strongly tempted to look at your paper to check what your pencil is doing.

Be strong, resist, don't look. As your eye literally inches along the contour, move your pencil at the same slow pace, always trying to feel the edge.

Remember, *don't* lift the pencil or look at the paper until you have finished the contour. If you are contouring a subject that has areas inside the contour and you wish to do them, lift your pencil, place it in the proper starting point and start again.

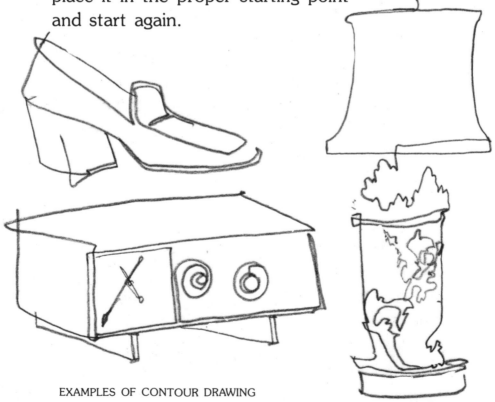

EXAMPLES OF CONTOUR DRAWING

This will teach you to *see* what you look at. It will also begin to discipline you to draw a clean direct line.

The result of these sessions may either make you despair or fall down laughing at what seem like ridiculous distortions. Laugh away but don't despair. Your drawings will improve with practice.

Gesture drawing. A gesture drawing is an extremely quick sketch — something like running half a mile (.805 km) as opposed to taking a long, slow walk. Use your largest pad or piece of paper and a soft — 2B or 4B — pencil or lead. Draw with quick, sweeping lines, seldom lifting your pencil from the paper.

In this exercise you want to show what the model is doing. Don't concern yourself with what

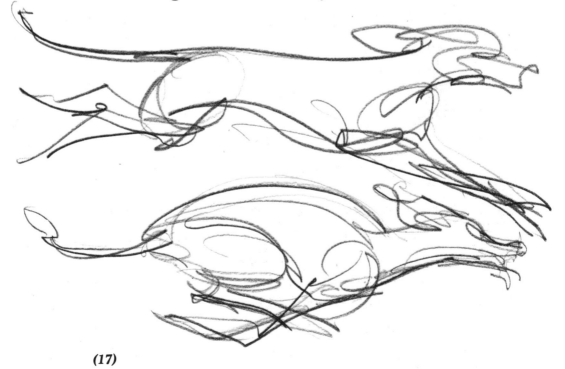

the model looks like, or even so much with what it is — but with what it is *doing*.

If you draw a dog running, don't worry that its head is not right. Just make sure you express the motion, so that when you look at it even if you don't know it's a dog, you won't be able to miss the forward rush of motion.

If you draw a person leaning over, concentrate on showing the curve of the head, the extended hand. Here again you don't lift your pencil off the surface. Let it move freely around the paper. Don't be concerned about detail. Doing the opposite of contour drawing, you don't try to follow the edges. Here you're reporting the *feeling* the subject gives you, not its precise form. In gesture drawing you are feeling the whole thing at once, not a piece at a time.

Important point. Do not use an eraser during either one of these sessions. These sessions are strictly training time. Save and date some of each type of drawing for future reference. At the end of two weeks of, say, twenty minutes a day, spread them out by date and see how you're doing.

(18)

Now you are faced with a more complex problem—the whole dog.

Most animal anatomical structure is basically a series of cylinders.

When looking at the muscle and hair that cover these forms, the beginning artist tends to become too engrossed in detail. Don't!

Remember to look *first* at your subject as a *whole* form. This should always rule your drawing observation. You will see that it is important in helping you understand light and shade.

The next four pages take up this problem as it arises when you do more finished sketches of the whole animal. Treat these pages as exercises. Go through each step separately. Your tracing paper will be excellent for this purpose.

Save the sketches for the separate steps. After every completed sketch review each step to find your strengths and your mistakes.

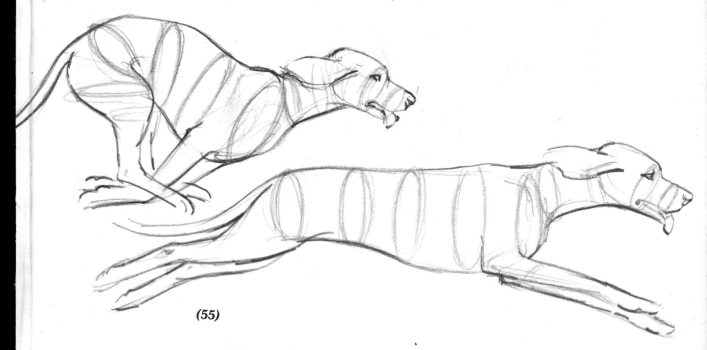

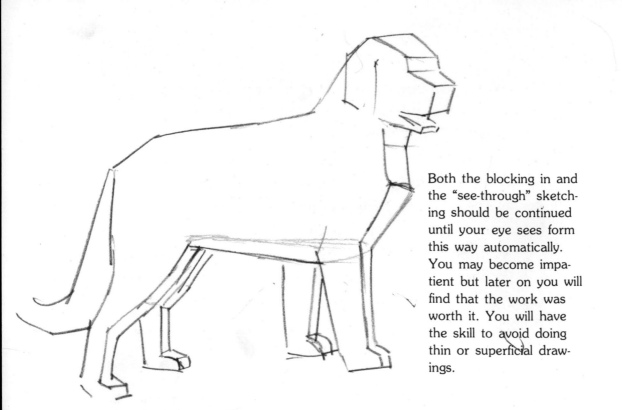

Both the blocking in and the "see-through" sketching should be continued until your eye sees form this way automatically. You may become impatient but later on you will find that the work was worth it. You will have the skill to avoid doing thin or superficial drawings.

The feeling you should strive for in this sketch of a Newfoundland is that of a heavy-set, big-boned, and powerful animal. If your refining sketch does not give that feeling, work on another until it expresses a sense of power and strength.

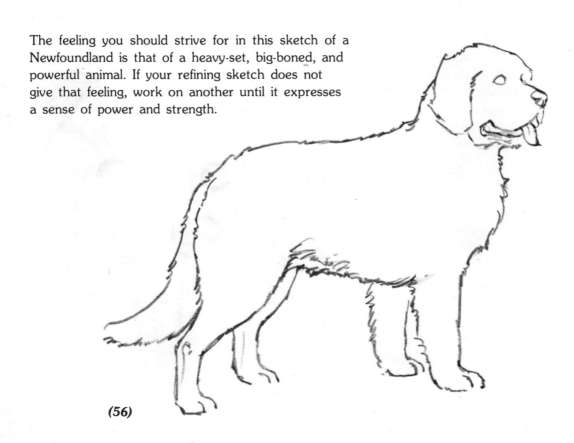

LIGHT SOURCE

Use this slightly different approach whenever your subject has light, shadow, and a two-toned coat. Plot your shaded areas first. Keep them simple. Then, when you've laid on the shadow and indication of hair growth, apply the tone to indicate the second color of the coat.

Another slightly different approach is used here and elsewhere when a long-haired dog is sketched. Normally a line as unbroken as possible gives greater clarity and strength to your sketch. In this sketch the line is quite frequently broken to give the feeling of a heavy coat. Try to do this every time you sketch a long-haired dog.

(57)

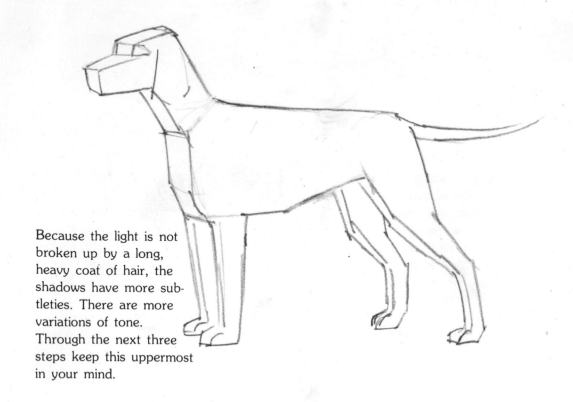

Because the light is not broken up by a long, heavy coat of hair, the shadows have more subtleties. There are more variations of tone. Through the next three steps keep this uppermost in your mind.

This is a hunting hound, a pointer, a very active type of dog. In your refining process strive for a hard, lean, and muscular look. Because of the short hair the muscular characteristics will be much more apparent.

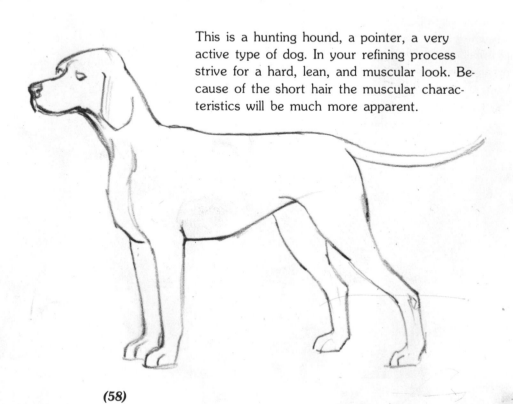

(58)

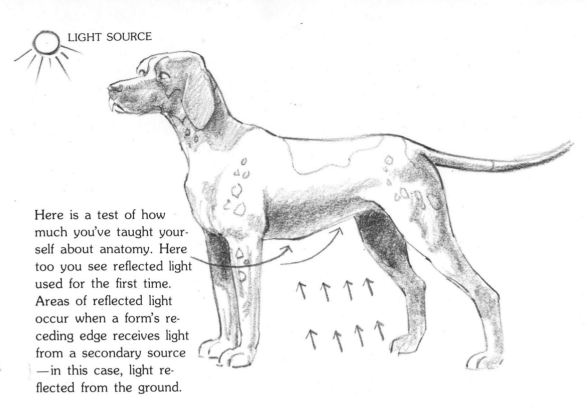

LIGHT SOURCE

Here is a test of how much you've taught your-self about anatomy. Here too you see reflected light used for the first time. Areas of reflected light occur when a form's re-ceding edge receives light from a secondary source —in this case, light re-flected from the ground.

Light hits the ground and is reflected up toward the surface facing it. This light is never as strong as the primary source.

As on pages 56 and 57, the hound's second color is the next to last tone to be laid on. This is to keep the job of shading as easy a progression as possible. The final tone will be the very dark or black areas you want for emphasis.

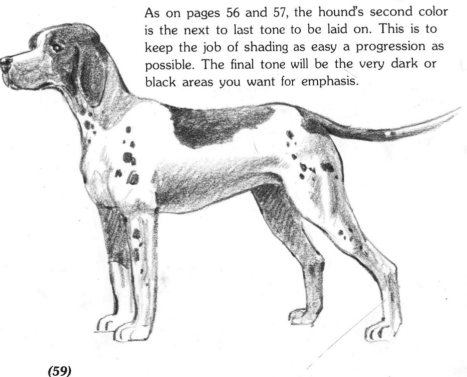

HUSKY

POODLE

BOXER

IRISH
WOLFHOUND

Chapter 6
Breeds of Dogs

There are over seventy-five distinct breeds of dogs. These breeds are separated into six general groups. These are sporting dogs, hounds, working dogs, terriers, nonsporting dogs, and toys.

Within these broad groups the various breeds may have two or more strains. A strain is a variation of a breed. A spaniel is a sporting dog, and within the spaniel group there are ten different strains. So if you like sketching dogs, you have an almost unlimited variety to choose from.

The next six pages and the facing page will give you a glimpse of some of the more popular breeds and a few less-usual ones.

**LONG-HAIRED
MIXED BREED**

GREAT DANE

The Great Dane is believed to have been developed in Germany and is probably a mixture of two breeds, the mastiff and the Irish wolfhound. It was originally bred to hunt wild boar and stands an impressive 30 inches (76.2 cm) or better at the shoulder. Its chest should be broad with a muscular body. In spite of its size and strength the Great Dane has a mild and friendly disposition.

COLLIE

The collie is one of the oldest breeds of dogs. It is thought to be of Scottish origin. It is a working breed, used mostly as a sheep dog, although it has been used successfully with cattle. Under a heavy, long-haired coat of black-and-tan or sable-with-white markings, it has a long, slim body with straight, strong legs. Collies are excellent with small children, probably because of their strong herding instinct and gentle disposition.

LABRADOR RETRIEVER

The Labrador retriever is a breed introduced in England from its native Newfoundland in the late 1800s. Its job is described by its name. It is a hunting dog that retrieves game that has been brought down on land or in water. A solidly built, well-muscled dog, it stands between 22 and 24 inches (55.9 and 61 cm) at the shoulder. Its black coat is short and very dense to give it protection against cold water. The Labrador retriever has a warm and gentle nature.

(64)

COCKER SPANIEL

The cocker spaniel is the smallest of the standard spaniels, standing about 12 inches (30.5 cm) at the shoulder and weighing between 18 and 20 pounds (8 and 9 kg). Its color variety is wider than in most other pure breeds, ranging from jet black to golden and several two-toned combinations. The cocker spaniel's most distinguishing features are very long ears and soulful eyes.

DACHSHUND

The name *Dachshund* means "badger dog," which describes the purpose for which it was bred in Germany. A keen sense of smell makes this dog ideal as a tracking dog. Despite its small size, about 19 inches (48 cm) and 12 pounds (5.5 kg), it has courage to spare. Careless breeding, however, has tended to weaken that trait in the American strain.

CAIRN TERRIER

This bright-eyed, spunky little fellow's ancestors started life in northwestern Scotland. It is a rugged little terrier, about 9 inches (22.9 cm) tall, and weighing 13 or 14 pounds (5.9 or 6.3 kg). As a working breed cairn terriers were tireless hunters of otters, foxes, and other small game. The cairn's outer coat of coarse, long hair covers an undercoat of soft fur which keeps it well protected in the harsh climate of its original habitat.

(67)

CORGI

COCKER SPANIEL

DALMATIAN

POODLE

Chapter 7
PUPPIES

Learning to draw puppies, to catch their characteristics, is more difficult than it appears.

Begin by observing carefully. Be sure what you see is not just looked at but truly observed and filed away in your mind. If you are fortunate enough to sketch from life, don't let early failures discourage you.

The first puppy quality to try for is its soft, rounded appearance. Nothing is sharp or as well defined as in the mature dog.

The second and equally important quality is the look they almost always have of being a little unsure, a touch off balance. As these are impressions rather than specifics, you'll be lucky if any of it comes easily.

JUST PLAIN PUPPY

This will be your first try at a group. Do just as you have with a sketch of a single dog. When you block in, try to imagine the whole of each of the two center puppies. Don't just copy the sketch.

If you'd rather, do each puppy as a single sketch. Then, working with your tracing paper, try to compose your own grouping. It would be excellent practice.

Here are some sketches of puppies for you to work from. Use them as models until you have your own photo file to work from. Certainly, if there's a chance to work from life, do so.

Good luck!

Here are several reminders. Make them daily habits, when you're not sketching.

Observe and file away in your mind, don't just look and pass on.

Sketch as frequently as you can. It helps you remember and makes you look beyond the surface. Keep your sketchbooks and date them.

If you have any problems that you feel I could be helpful with, write to me in care of the publisher and I'll be happy to help if possible. Have fun.

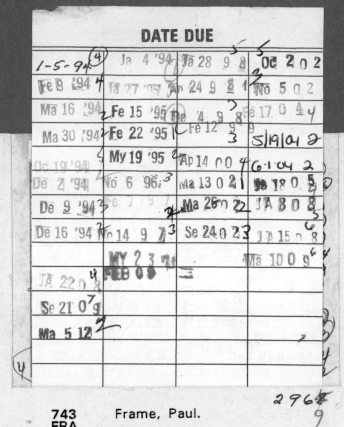